THIS IS NO LONGER THE PROPERTY
OF THE SEATTLE PUBLIC LIBRARY

SEATTLE ....From Where I See It

PHOTOGRAPHS BY

DOUG TOSTENSON

FROM WHERE I SEE IT
PUBLISHING
SEATLE

DISTRIBUTION AND PUBLISHING
FROM WHERE I SEE IT LLC
3429 BURKE AVENUE NORTH, #21
SEATTLE, WASHINGTON 98103

WWW.FROMWHEREISEEIT.COM

PHOTOGRAPHS COPYRIGHT / 2012 DOUG TOSTENSON

ALL RIGHTS RESERVED. NO PART OF THIS BOOK MAY BE
REPRODUCED IN ANY FORM WITHOUT WRITTEN PERMISSION FROM
THE PUBLISHER.

ISBN# 978-0-9849725-0-0

FIRST EDITION

PRINT AND COLOR MANAGEMENT BY IOCOLOR, SEATTLE

PRINTED IN CHINA BY SHENZHEN ARTRON COLOR PRINTING LTD

SPECIAL THANKS

TO

LEXI MANDELSTAM

An artistic journey through the streets of Seattle

" Soft Blue City "

" VIADUCT DRIVE "

" Waterfront "

" THE BEND "

" THE MARKET "

" Two Stacks "

" Sunday Morning "

" Very Cool Day "

" Seattle Night "

" PARMOUNT THEATRE "

" In Town "

" THE ALLEY "

" Seattle Art Museum "

" Lake of Union "

" Ballard Locks "

" The Aurora Bridge "

" Fremont Snow "

" Behind The Scene "

" Man on Paddleboard "

" Safeco Field "

" Elliott Bay "

" University Bridge "

" Pike Place "

" Smith Tower "

" CITY STUDY "

" Afternoon Waterfront "

" Metropolis "

" 1st & Pike "

" Only "